Guidelines

for effective teams

by
Kaley Warner Klemp

For Jim Warner, who taught so many of us the original guidelines.

Published and distributed by
Kaley Warner Klemp
4040 Joelton Drive
Agoura Hills, CA 91301
www.kaleyklemp.com

Contact us for information on author interviews, speaking engagements or team retreats.

First Edition, 2010

PUBLISHER'S CALALOGUING-IN-PUBLICATION DATA
Klemp, Kaley, 1979 –
13 guidelines for effective teams

ISBN – 978-0615518657
1. Group facilitation – Handbooks, manuals, etc
2. Business meetings – Handbooks, manuals, etc
3. Leadership

Published in the United States of America
Set in Adobe Caslon Pro
Designed by Evan Lange

Foreword

By Jim Warner

After fifteen years of working in small group settings, I continue to be amazed and baffled by the insidious power of the human ego. The unchecked ego can cause us to detach or dominate; to complain or blame; to conceal or smother; to withdraw and compare; to hold resentment or seek recognition. In these and other forms the ego both drains energy and inhibits productivity in groups.

Some people, but not very many, have an innate governor that monitors their ego and allows them to be open and collaborative, even in high-pressure situations. Most of us, when the stakes are high or emotion is present, have no such governor. Instead, when feelings are strong, we tend to fall into self-righteous or self-defeating behaviors that block creativity and compromise our relationships.

The ego needs some clear rules-of-engagement for safe and synergistic interactions in small groups. Kaley's guidelines provide exactly that—a succinct and proven framework for authenticity. They remind group members to take full responsibility for their lives and to show up with a blend of compassion, candor and courage. They breed an environment of mutual trust, integrity, and tenderness, where group participants can be truthful with one another, offering counsel, holding one another accountable, and pointing out blind spots.

These guidelines aren't just "theory." Kaley and her colleagues have used them in hundreds of group settings... and they work. With these guidelines as a foundation, we've witnessed groups who were stuck in passive, transactional, or sabotaging behaviors transform into creative, collaborative, caring groups of peers, committed to authentic interactions.

I urge you to adopt them in all areas of your life.

Jim Warner

July 2010

Introduction

I spend my time working with groups of every sort – executive teams, YPO forums, families and couples. Whenever I begin a session, I always start with guidelines. They facilitate collaboration by making the group a safe place to share ideas, communicate and give feedback. Guidelines ensure common understanding so that we can accomplish the real goals of the session. And, when maintained over time, having a solid set of guidelines is a key factor for successful group interactions.

The definition of these guidelines shifts slightly in different settings. In this book, I focus on the use of guidelines with teams in organizations. You can imagine how you could take these same guidelines and apply them elsewhere — or at least how you could have a conversation about how they apply to a personal relationship, volunteer board, or other collaborative setting.

You can use this set of guidelines at any level in your organization. Modeling the guidelines yourself is a good first step; teaching them to everyone you expect to use them is crucial if they are to become an established part of your culture.

While 13 guidelines may initially seem like a lot, they flow into one another to cover multiple aspects of interpersonal relationships. I've tried reducing the list, only to find the group needed the one I cut. I've tested these guidelines with thousands of leaders. They work. May they become a backdrop to your success.

Sincerely,

Kaley Warner Klemp

Guidelines

I Will Respect Confidentiality

The key to this first guideline is defining confidentiality clearly. Young Presidents' Organization, a premier global leadership network for CEOs and Presidents of companies, defines confidentiality as "nothing, no one, never." This means that information shared in a forum group stays confidential indefinitely.

Different groups require different levels of confidentiality. Some groups manage sensitive information – personal, professional or organizational. For example, consider the various levels of confidentiality that might be required for a compensation committee, a team working on an acquisition or a group leading a new product launch. All of these groups may require varying degrees of confidentiality ranging from "closed-door" to "transparent."

The compensation committee may decide that salary and bonus decisions always remain confidential. Or, they may create an environment of "open books," where once decisions are made, everyone has access to the information. The decision is not as important as every person having the same expectation and commitment.

COMMON AREAS FOR BREACHES IN CONFIDENTIALITY:

Spouses. Be very clear whether the information can or cannot be shared with spouses or significant others. Once the network of people with the information expands, it becomes more difficult to manage. Those not committed to the guidelines may not share your definition of confidentiality.

Email. Typically all email exchanges are stored on a server somewhere. As recent lawsuits have shown, email is not private or confidential.

Good intentions. In my experience, I have very rarely seen breaches of confidentiality with a malicious intent. More often, someone is trying to help.

The consequences of breaking confidentiality can be severe, from a rise or drop in stock price due to news of an acquisition to personal reputational damage. Sometimes a breach of confidentiality may seem unimportant, but a violation of confidentiality always undermines trust.

In a discussion of confidentiality it is important to remember that your information and experiences belong to you. Your willingness to be transparent with your own experience – feeling comfortable revealing your stories – frees you from requiring confidentiality to the same degree.

That said, as part of a corporate team, keeping business information confidential avoids business drama. And, other people's information isn't yours to share anyway.

ex.

If Joe wants to look for a new job and tells his colleague Fred in confidence, Fred will need to ask Joe how he can help within their confidentiality agreement. Is he able to share this information with a friend who is a headhunter? Can Fred mention Joe's name if someone asks if he has recommendations for a job opening?

At first glance, it would seem like both of these would help Joe. On second thought, if the headhunter is friends with Joe's boss (which Fred may not know) and mentions that Joe is looking, it could negatively impact Joe's current career.

The moral of all confidentiality stories: Be very careful to define your confidentiality agreements before you help someone on a confidential issue.

TAKE-AWAY

When in doubt, err on the side of confidentiality – the consequences are worth the caution.

DISCUSSION QUESTIONS:

• What is your team's agreement about confidentiality?

• Precisely what can you share? And with whom?

I Will Be Present
In the Moment

According to 2009 research by Dukette and Cornish, the average human attention span is 8 seconds. This means that every 8 seconds something besides what you are currently doing vies for your attention. With this fact in mind, it is easy to see why remaining focused for an entire meeting – or even a complete conversation – is so challenging!

By committing to be present in the moment, you become responsible for resisting the temptation to let your attention wander. Instead, you stay with the topic at hand, engaging fully in the present moment.

This guideline is especially important during meetings and conversations. Multi-tasking has become a popular pastime and often a perceived necessity. But research seems conclusive that it doesn't actually work. You cannot be focused on two things at once. The statistics for car accidents are alarmingly high when you are doing something else: eating, talking on the phone, or texting. Even if your eyes are on the road, if your attention is fragmented your driving is compromised.

While your multi-tasking at work may not result in a dented fender, misunderstandings and project delays are good evidence that splitting your attention is ineffective. By bringing your attention to the moment, you show respect, a fundamental quality of strong cultures. Equally important, you are more efficient and productive when you are mentally attentive and focused.

COMMON WAYS TO LOSE PRESENCE:

1. Cell phones. When any email or phone device (Blackberry, iPhone, cell or PDA) vibrates in your pocket or on your waist, your attention immediately shifts to the device. Even if you don't answer the call or look at the message, the distraction prevents full engagement with the person you are actually with.

The easy solution: put your phone on silent when you are meeting with another person.

2. E-mail notifications on the computer. If your email makes a sound each time it receives a message, it virtually guarantees that you will never fully concentrate in your office. The noise pulls your attention to the e-mail rather than letting you focus on the person sitting across from you, your research, writing, analysis, strategy session, materials to consolidate, brainstorming session or any productive work. Even leaving the program open while you are trying to work can interrupt your thought process each time a new message arrives.

The easy solution: turn off email alarms and read your e-mail at designated time intervals.

3. Remembering things. If you don't write things down, you have to keep reminding yourself of them. The human memory requires periodic (and quite frequent!) refreshes. So, in order to keep from missing something on your to-do list, you have to keep thinking about it. This keeps you from focusing fully on what you are doing.

The easy solution: carry around something to capture your thoughts and to-dos. It can be a small notebook, an area of your smart phone or the back of your hand. It doesn't matter so long as you can put it somewhere safe so it is out of your mind. Then you can focus on the content of your current interaction.

TIPS FOR BEING PRESENT IN THE MOMENT

Take a deep breath

You can only breathe in the present. You can't breathe yesterday or breathe tomorrow. Taking the time to take a deep breath helps you get centered in what you are doing now.

Make eye contact

To stay present in the moment with another person, focus your body and eyes on them.

Schedule breaks

Knowing that the human attention span is limited, schedule intentional breaks in your workday or meeting. Every 60-90 minutes, spend 5 minutes moving. Stretch. Walk around. Get a glass of water. Building in time for your brain to recharge on purpose helps keep it focused when you need it!

TAKE-AWAY

You are your most impactful when your attention is fully focused on what you are doing right now – when you are present in the moment.

DISCUSSION QUESTIONS

• What distracts you the most?

• What helps you stay present in the moment?

I Will Stay Around
When Times Get Tough

Just as a real fan is measured by his loyalty during a losing season, real dedication to a team or organization happens when you weather a storm together. This guideline reminds people to tap into their courage. When each person on the team is committed to stay through tough times, it facilitates the sharing of challenging information like "we've uncovered fraud" or "a key customer is unhappy."

Most people are willing to raise difficult issues when they feel confident that someone else will be there to help solve the problem. The primary importance of this guideline is to ensure commitment from all team members, so that everyone engages fully until completion.

When each person stays around when times get tough, the team creates resolutions. As the team below will demonstrate, their commitment to follow this guideline allowed them to come to resolutions they never would have reached without it.

ex.

I was about to lead an offsite retreat for a start-up company when a woman from the company called me. "I'm not sure I can come on the offsite," she said. "I'm worried that if I raise my concerns, the team will fall apart." This group needed the guideline, "I will stay around when times get tough." She needed to know that the team would reach completion, not stop when things were difficult.

During our meeting, I intentionally spent time with the group on this guideline. I emphasized that when the situation is most challenging is when the team needs everyone's full commitment. The woman who called had concerns about the use of borderline accounting practices in the company. What she discovered by speaking her truth (I'll elaborate on this in Guideline 5) is that others had similar doubts – but about misleading promotional materials and unfulfilled promises to customers.

Through clear, sometimes pointed, conversations, this team was able to identify the source of the problem (which actually turned out to be multiple problems) and take steps to resolve each of them. There were several moments when it seemed the easier path would have been to quit – to let the company and team dissolve. But, because everyone committed to stay around when times got tough, they were able to construct effective solutions for very difficult problems.

As I debriefed the offsite with various team members, they said they had suspected months before the offsite many of the problems that were discussed. But only when they shared a *commitment* to stay around when times got tough could they have this crucial conversation.

If you are like most people, you have defense mechanisms to protect you when topics move to an area where you feel uncomfortable – you "check out." When times get tough, sometimes not "staying around" means literally removing yourself from the environment. More often, people use more subtle forms of "checking out."

You may find your "favorite" mode in the list below, or have a unique way to keep yourself from staying engaged.

Staying around instead of "checking out" becomes particularly important in meetings where the group has discussed various options and each option has a flaw. It would be easy to slip into any of these "check out" modes. Instead, stay committed to finding a creative solution.

To prevent disengaging in tough times, teams can do an exercise to identify situations where they would be likely to "check out." Members may choose from the list in this book, or name their own. Each person shares his or her default disengagement strategy. The truly courageous can then ask others in the group for feedback on their behavior: whether others see another form of "checking out" that they missed.

COMMON MODES OF "CHECKING OUT":

- Thinking about your to-do list
- Daydreaming
- Cracking a joke
- Changing the subject
- Deflecting attention
- Needing to use the restroom – right now
- Getting defensive
- Getting very tired, too tired to concentrate
- Giving up / not caring
- Taking a victim stance (it's not my fault)
- Becoming aggressive (best defense is a good offense)
- Turning cynical

Just knowing the risky scenarios – when each person on the team is most likely to disengage – helps groups monitor their dynamics and reengage if attention starts to slip. Some groups invite other members to catch them checking out. They then use one other as accountability coaches to return to the discussion – to stay around when times get tough.

TAKE-AWAY

Make an early personal and team commitment to stay around when times get tough, so you can address challenges and solve problems with the confidence of team support.

DISCUSSION QUESTIONS

- What topic have you avoided because you lacked confidence the team was committed to staying around to solve it?

- What's your role in addressing it now?

4

I Will Be on Time and Stay Until the End

Nowhere are egos tested and displayed with more drama than in the realm of punctuality and time commitments. Time is about integrity and respect. When you honor time commitments, you reinforce your own integrity and respect for others. The message you convey when you are late is that you think your time is more important than everyone else's.

ex.

I sat in the meeting room and looked at the clock. It was the agreed time to begin, but only five of the nine members of the team were there. I sat, observing the culture of the team. Within the next 10 minutes, three additional members strolled in – relieved to not be the last into the room, grateful they had not wasted time waiting for others.

Fifteen minutes past the start time, Sara was still missing. I asked the group what they normally do with their meetings, whether they wanted me to wait for Sara. "She's an important decision maker," they said, "We have to wait."

So the team sat waiting for Sara for 20 minutes. Individuals brought out their computers, checked their voicemail, and chatted with each other. Finally, Sara entered the room with a cursory apology. "Traffic," she offered.

Her team members rolled their eyes or exchanged glances with each other.

The team looked at me to begin. Rather than starting with the original agenda, I asked the team, "How are you feeling right now?"

"Frustrated and angry," they admitted.

It took a concerted effort – time spent addressing the unspoken issues that had arisen due to the "permission" of tardiness – to get past the resentment that had built on the team. The team stayed engaged, even through tough exchanges. When we concluded, the team was committed to be on time and stay until the end.

Teams that have clear agreements about time are more productive, efficient and happy than those who do not.

If you are serious about implementing this guideline, the first responsibility is to model timeliness. Whether you're the leader of the team, the department, or the company – or just leading the meeting – if you want others to be on time, you must arrive on time, and start the meeting on time. Whether everyone is there or not, begin on time.

Do not re-cap information. If people miss the first 10 minutes of the meeting, they miss the first 10 minutes of content; it has already been covered and will not be repeated. Make your meeting like a plane: if you are late, it leaves without you.

The second responsibility is to manage the time well. Design an efficient agenda so that the meeting lasts only as long as it needs to. People stay until the end when meetings finish on time.

The final responsibility is to ensure that the meeting is worthwhile. Being on time and staying until the end is a measure of respect. It is also a measure of value. Think about the last time you went to see a speaker you admired. You wanted to hear every word – and you arranged your schedule accordingly – because you predetermined the message would be valuable to you. Your job when you lead a meeting is to make the content so important that people want to be at your meeting as much as you wanted to hear that esteemed speaker.

TAKE-AWAY

When you are on time, you show respect. When you treat time as a valued asset, it is used well.

DISCUSSION QUESTION

• What would you need to do to create a norm of punctuality in your organization and in your life?

I Will Speak
My Truth

As Benjamin Franklin said, honesty is the best policy. On effective teams, each person is both empowered and expected to speak his or her truth. This guideline does not mean that you will reveal everything about you. There may be details of your personal life that you choose to keep private. But, when asked about a topic, the agreement is to speak your truth.

In some instances, your truth may be, "I'd prefer not to talk about it." And your truth may be, "I have some doubts that I have not volunteered." According to this agreement, though, if someone asks about the product, you would not say, "It's fine," if you have reservations. Instead, you are committed to honesty with everything you say.

Additionally, this guideline encourages you to reach for your deepest truth. Honesty is one level. Revealing is another. If you have the same thought three times, it is worth revealing. Your strength as a leader increases when you develop self-awareness and find more authentic truths. This happens when you move from perceptions of others to truths about yourself. These truths may be prompted by your reaction to someone else or your response to a situation. And when you can stay with it and find the deeper truth about you, a path opens to more genuine conversation and collaboration opportunities.

For instance, an initial level of truth might be, "I don't think you're doing your job." Stretching to the next level – truth about you – the more authentic statement might be, "I feel scared that this isn't getting done."

I have coached many leaders in conflict with one another, where embracing *my truth* made all the difference. Time after time, as the individuals spoke their deeper truths, the conversation shifted from variations on, "There's something wrong with you," to "I feel angry, sad or scared because I don't know what to do here."

There is an important distinction here – your truth is not **the** truth. You can only see the world through your own eyes. You can only report the story as you see it or understand it. You can only speak **your** truth. By being clear about this distinction, the conversation remains open, allowing healthy debate or discussion.

As a leader, you cannot punish others for expressing differing perspectives. If there are negative consequences for having a conflicting opinion or articulating a concern, people typically stop raising questions. Inviting each person, both through words and action, "Please, speak your truth," prevents the "I told you so" phenomenon. As long as every person on the team follows the guideline, you can trust that you know all points of view. You won't find out later that there were reservations that were never voiced.

ex.

I worked with a team with a brilliant, forward-looking CEO who we'll call Sam. The team was inspired to act quickly and boldly, but also felt intimidated to raise challenges with him. Somehow along the way, the team embraced that Sam's way was *the* way. While it often led to success, the team rarely challenged him, which meant he made mistakes that could have been avoided.

When we practiced this guideline as a team, Sam made clear that he welcomed other perspectives. He acknowledged that his truth was just *his* perspective and challenges enhanced everyone's thinking. The team entered a new era of candor and clarity – which led to impressive results.

Learn to separate *your* truth from *the* truth.

DISCUSSION QUESTIONS

- What truth of yours have you been withholding?

- What has kept you from revealing it?

- How could you share it?

I Will Ask for
What I Want

I have yet to meet a person with the ability to flawlessly read minds. In the absence of ESP, you are responsible to ask for what you want. This doesn't mean that you will necessarily get it. But by clearly asking, you increase drastically the potential that you could get what you want.

Someone may try to foresee what you want – and sometimes that works. More often than not, the person guesses wrong. Your need is still unfulfilled, and the person who anticipated the need feels frustrated that he or she worked for nothing.

In organizations that follow this guideline, the culture shifts out of complaining and gossip. Consider that instead of complaining about something, you have the responsibility to make a request for how things can change. This simple shift creates profound results as each individual takes ownership for shaping his or her experiences and environment.

Additionally, *I will ask for what I want* facilitates more effective conversations. When requests are clear, changes happen faster and more valuable topics are covered. For instance, "I'd like to change the subject," "I want to move on," or "I want to revisit a prior decision" all move the conversation forward in a productive manner. This is faster and more valuable than waiting, pouting or complaining. Sometimes the request is denied, but at least desires are clear.

If you are not able to (or choose not to) grant someone else's request, you can cleanly set the boundary. If you (or someone on your team) has the courage to make a request, the appropriate response is an honest answer. When both people speak their truths (from the previous guideline) and ask for what they want, typically a workable, often creative, solution emerges for both parties.

ex.

I worked with a team offsite where Bill, a reluctant attendee, started complaining about the room choice. "It doesn't have any windows," he began. "The HVAC is too loud. It's not spacious enough. My chair is uncomfortable…" he continued his lament.

I interrupted, "So, Bill, what do you want?" He stopped in his tracks. As soon as he realized that he would need to shift his complaints to an actionable request, his tone shifted. "I want to work outside, so we can take advantage of the beautiful day."

"Working outside isn't an option for the content we cover in this program," I said. "But, we could consider regular breaks, where you could go outside."

At this point, the discussion ensued to find a solution that worked for Bill and was also appropriate for the session. The turning point was when Bill stopped complaining, and instead made a request. He didn't get exactly what he wanted, but he learned a valuable lesson about asking for what he wanted – and also about taking responsibility for making his requests become reality. His reluctance transformed.

At the next offsite, Bill was engaged. He took charge of the logistics, and the team met me in a space that was completely private (conducive to the confidential content of the meeting), and also outside on a shaded balcony. It was a creative, workable solution for all!

This guideline to *ask for what you want* also facilitates opportunities. For instance, you might ask to be part of a new cross-functional team so you can learn new skills and grow professionally. Or, you might decline placement on the cross-functional team so you can focus on your area of expertise, where you believe you add the most value. One option may look more attractive to you than to someone else. Since the only person who knows what you want is you, you must make the request.

ex.

> While working with a team, the all-star employee confided in me that he was upset at the quantity of work he was doing. "I work every weekend and most nights past 11pm. This is unsustainable!" When I asked him if he had made a request to HR for additional personnel, he confessed he hadn't. "I don't want to sound like I'm complaining," he admitted.
>
> In our session, we discussed the guideline *I will ask for what I want.* In conjunction with *I will speak my truth,* the employee expressed that he wanted to start looking for an additional person for his team. The HR person was grateful to have the request — now she could recruit for the position needed, rather than replacing a star who burned out.

As illustrated in the story, people often need to be reminded to ask for help when they need it. This is a subset of the guideline *I will ask for what I want.* If you need collaboration from another person, or support from another function, it is important to ask (rather than be stoic or complain). Again, sometimes others volunteer; more often they need to be asked.

As a manager, you can coach your team to ask for what they want, which usually makes your job easier. You can respond to real needs rather than complaints. You can offer your assistance when necessary. Or, you can encourage the person to fulfill the requirement on his or her own.

Sometimes you can help a person see the root desire beneath a request. The person may ask for something, but when you think about it, there is something else that would address the situation better. You can appreciate a person for asking. Then you can ask, what do you really want?

ex.

I was coaching a team where a manager named Sue had to go to another department head on a weekly (sometimes daily) basis to get a piece of information. Sue was frustrated because when the department head was busy, Sue had to wait or send follow-up e-mails to get her need met. Finally, Sue asked the department head to be responsive to her calls. When Sue and the department head explored the request, what Sue really wanted was access to the information so she could get it herself on her own timeline. The department head created a new access portal for Sue – which was much less time consuming for both of them.

By stretching to the root desire, Sue found a much more elegant solution for both parties.

When you follow the guideline *I will ask for what I want,* you are more likely to get it. As a leader, when you empower others to ask for what they want, you get information and guidance that allows you to make decisions faster. As Mick Jagger of *The Rolling Stones* wisely said, "You can't always get what you want. But if you try sometimes, you just might find, you get what you need."

6

No one can read your mind. Ask for what you want.

DISCUSSION QUESTIONS

• What keeps you from asking for what you want?

• Who do you need to ask, "What do *you* want?"

I Will Take
Care of Myself

I have sometimes tried to combine this guideline with *I will ask for what I want* or *I will speak my truth*. It is intimately connected to both of these guidelines. Still, because it is so common in groups, I have found it worthwhile to separate it into its own guideline.

I will take care of myself means that every person on the team honors their own needs with the same attention they would give to those of others. If you need sleep to think clearly, healthy food to be physically energized, or a break from a conflict to gather your thoughts, it is your responsibility to make sure you get what you need.

Have you ever worked yourself to the point of exhaustion? Or skipped a meal because you were completing a project? Have you stopped exercising because you couldn't seem to find the time? Or found that your social connections started to suffer? These are common ways individuals do not take care of themselves. This guideline invites you into responsibility for your self-care.

Taking care of yourself is different from being selfish. This does not mean that you follow whims without discernment or put your own desires ahead of the company. Instead, it means that you will take care of yourself such that you can give your best in your own work, to your colleagues and in your life.

Following this guideline also does not mean you forfeit the ability to be cared for. Welcoming others' assistance and feedback can be one of the most powerful aspects of a team. Since people receive help differently, each person must take responsibility for making sure his or her needs are met.

ex.

I was working with a group where Andy, a team leader, resisted taking time to present his challenges. "I don't want to take the group's time for addressing an issue I should be able to fix on my own. I feel better when I'm able to help others; I don't want to be selfish."

When I asked Andy whether the team was meeting his needs, he realized that he had been refusing assistance. By refusing to be taken care of, he was not taking care of himself. He opened to the possibility that welcoming others' ideas – letting them help him – was not selfish, but increased the collaborative and problem-solving powers of the team.

This guideline is a favorite for leaders. It's one of my personal favorites when I work with groups because it relieves me of the self-imposed burden of taking care of everyone else. When I share this guideline, I remind teams that they know when they need a break or when they have exhausted a topic. For every leader, it is not your job to protect others from themselves. You can care for them without caretaking and rescuing. You can coach and teach without doing someone else's work.

For example, in groups where I facilitate, every exercise is an invitation. I encourage full participation – I find it to be true that you get out what you put in – and respect when a person chooses not to partake. Since I trust each person to take care of him or herself, they trust me more as a leader. I encourage everyone to participate at the level they are willing. I am very careful to say "willing" and not "comfortable" because so much growth happens outside a person's comfort zone. Ironically, since I do not force anyone to do anything, I find participants in my offsites, retreats, meetings, and workshops are willing to try more things. And they do so knowing that they are in control of their own needs.

Back at the office, teams notice they can make requests of one another, trusting that the other person will *appropriately* accept or decline. Mandates and assignments may still be necessary, this just ensures that the outcome is balanced with the cost (personally, energetically, etc). Productivity grows as members take care of themselves, bringing even more energy to the team and projects.

TAKE-AWAY

When you take care of yourself you bring out your best, which benefits all those around you.

DISCUSSION QUESTIONS

- Who or what do you care for above yourself?

- What are the consequences of that action?

- How can you take better care of yourself?

- How could you open to more care from others?

8

I Will Listen With Curiosity and Openness

Most of the guidelines are about how you participate and interact with others. This guideline is about how you commit to receive others' contributions to you.

Most people want to say things with tact. And, in effective groups, people share comments from a place of wanting to help rather than hurt the other person. Yet, the person receiving the feedback makes the final decision for how they react and interpret it.

I often do an entire session with groups on the power of curiosity. The essence is this - in every situation you get to choose between two alternatives: curiosity and defensiveness.

When you choose curiosity, you choose learning. This commitment to *learn* defines managers, leaders and the most effective teams. Curiosity allows to you create superior results because you have more data points available; you can be nimble, adapting to new circumstances and growing from feedback to ultimately improve.

This is in contrast to defensiveness. When you choose defensiveness, you choose to be *right* above all else.

What feedback could be offered that would be valuable if you are *right?* There's nothing more to learn; there's no reason to explore or grow. You have already made up your mind. You are already convinced. From the defensive posture of being *right,* you have limited your learning and growth.

As discussed before, you can rarely be absolutely sure you are right. The most you have is your truth. If you are closed to any other inputs, it can be a lonely place. If you already have all the answers, you don't really have a need for a group or team.

Committing to curiosity and openness in every situation can feel risky. After all, when every situation is a learning experience, there is a lot more to learn.

Each time I share this concept with a team, someone raises the question, "What if I really am right? Do I have to agree with the person's feedback in order to be curious?"

The short answer is, "No." There is a difference between curiosity and agreement.

Consider the following example: in many companies where I have worked, leaders benefit from receiving 360 feedback. This is a chance for everyone in a company – superiors (boss, board, customers), peers (other team members) and direct reports – to provide anonymous feedback to a selected individual regarding areas to sustain, change and develop. These results are consolidated, looking for themes and areas of significant concern. Based on this feedback, I coach the executive to set an individualized growth plan.

ex.

> With one company that did 360 feedback, an executive received feedback that his leadership style was tyrannical.
>
> "Of course I'm tyrannical!" he retorted. "Do you know what would happen if I wasn't always in control? What would happen if consequences for mistakes weren't harsh?? This company would be unruly; I have to rule with an iron fist!"
>
> Notice that he agreed with the feedback he received (the feedback was right): he was tyrannical. But, since he was committed to defending his behavior (his way was the right way), and was closed to other options, he couldn't see which aspects of control were necessary to run the company and which were stifling the progress of his people. His defensiveness was preventing his company's success and his own growth.

On the opposite extreme, a different executive received feedback that he was overly protective of his people.

"Really?" he asked. "I never would have thought that would be the case. That's definitely not my intent. I wonder what I'm doing that's being misperceived as favoritism or paternalism."

He didn't agree with the feedback (he thought that by objective measures he was *right* in how he managed his people amidst the larger company). And, he was <u>still</u> curious about his role in creating this situation. He was open to change, if he just knew how. And he was committed to getting ideas to understand what behaviors he needed to modify in order to remedy the problem. His curiosity invited additional feedback so he could align his intentions with others' perceptions. He learned and grew so much from the experience that his company began to thrive even more.

Being curious does not mean giving up expertise, prior experience or convictions. It means being open to alternatives. There is a difference between holding a position and defensiveness. You can hold a position and stay connected with the other person, seeking to understand their point of view. Your body language stays open (posture, eye contact, breathing). Your tone stays engaged. Your thoughts stay with the ideas being presented, rather than composing your retort. You can see your beliefs, and hold them lightly – you could even let them go.

It's possible that the way you've always done an activity could be more efficient. Or that the approach you've always taken to earning new customers could be more persuasive. Or, your current preferences may be industry standard. When you are curious, you can hold all this information and still welcome a new perspective.

The highest commitment in curiosity is to learn. Innovation is reserved for those curious enough to pursue the uncharted path, to try the new way – to receive feedback and adjust. The greatest leaders welcome feedback in any form it is given.

8

Curiosity is a commitment to learn and an avenue for growth.

DISCUSSION QUESTIONS

- When do you react defensively?

- What are your tell-tale signs that you are defensive? (Body language, interrupting, passive-aggressiveness, stubbornness, etc.)

I Will Own
My Judgments

In most groups, this guideline, *I will own my judgments* gets the most questions. I think this happens because judgment has a negative connotation for many people in Western culture. Many children are taught not to be judgmental. So many people – especially if they are making an effort to be polite – shy away from having judgments at all. The problem is that people have judgments all the time. Judging is one of the primary "jobs" people have. In fact, consider that you are judging the value of this book *right now*.

As you determine whether you agree or disagree with the suggestions I offer, you are making a judgment. When you compare your experiences with those I share here, you are judging. Even deciding whether something here is right for you involves making a judgment. All of this is to say, judgments aren't bad – they just need to be acknowledged and owned.

This guideline is a very important governor for communication. Judgment is a synonym for opinion, thought and perception. The capability to judge is crucial to making choices in life. Without it, people would lose the ability to discern – to choose one path over another, or to make a recommendation to a boss, colleague or friend.

Once you welcome judgments and opinions into your dialogue, the key is to differentiate them from facts. Much like the guideline *I will speak my truth* requires the acknowledgment that *my* truth may be different from someone else's, this guideline requires the distinction between a judgment and an objective fact.

A judgment, or any of its synonyms, describes the meaning you assign to a set of information. People commonly confuse a judging statement with facts. For instance, you cannot say, "The fact is, it's hot!" It may be 90 degrees, but it is only your *judgment* that it is hot. Having recently spent time in India in late May, 90 degrees can be wonderfully cool – at least that is my judgment.

A phrase that works well with teams is "I make up a story that…" This clearly separates the "what happened" from "what I make it mean." Stories are often based in fact, but are themselves fiction. The only thing true about a judgment is that I believe it.

For example, if a person doesn't return two of my phone calls within 3 days, I could make it mean that they are rude, that they aren't interested in collaborating with me, or that they are extremely busy and haven't had time to call back yet. Any of these stories might be accurate. All I know for certain is that I haven't received a return call. The rest are stories. The more clear I can be in my own mind separating factual events from my stories about them, the more effectively I will be able to communicate with others.

If I were to confront the other person about not returning my calls, I would want to be very clear in my presentation:

"When I didn't hear back from either of my calls after 3 days, *(factual event)* I made up that it meant you were ignoring me *(story)*."

This conversation will be much more effective than starting with the assumption that my judgment is right (i.e., *"Why are you ignoring me?"*).

A primary value of working in teams is that results typically improve when there are more perspectives and ideas. The ability to respectfully challenge one another increases the chances of making good decisions. Additionally, having other people whose opinion you trust allows you to learn more about yourself.

Consider for a moment the last time you saw the back of your own head. Many people report that it was when they got their hair cut – in the mirror. If you think about it, you can't see the back of your own head with just one mirror – it requires two.

Similarly, for you to see the limitations of your own perspective often takes the reflections of two other people. In the same way mirrors are only helpful if they reflect accurately (unlike the ones at the carnival fun house), team member perceptions only help when they are honest – when they are *speaking their truth*.

In teams where members give each other candid feedback, owning judgments becomes even more important.

ex.

Imagine that you have been working on a project at work that has had you at the office until 9pm each night for the last month, so you have missed dinner with your family. If I were offering you feedback, after establishing the facts, I might say, "I'd like to share a judgment about your recent work schedule." Because this is personal, and potentially sensitive territory, I might re-emphasize that I know this is just my judgment. "This is just my opinion. I know that it may or may not be right."

Then I could proceed with the feedback with both people knowing the conversation is meant to provide perspective, without believing that it is true. The judgment is offered to assist, without attachment to being right. "I think that you have been working too much recently. I'm concerned that missing dinner every night for a month is unfair to your family." The hope is that by sharing this judgment, I am able to help this other person.

Sharing judgments of this sort requires that both people are committed to curiosity from the prior guideline.

The unwritten rule that makes this guideline work is a concept we call *Plexiglas*. The product *Plexiglas* is clear like glass, but indestructible like plastic. The idea is that the person on the receiving end of the judgment has a *Plexiglas* shield. Unlike a shield of armor that is designed to be impenetrable, a *Plexiglas* shield allows team members to receive the feedback, shift to curiosity and consider it while protecting their feelings. It serves to prevent hurt feelings by slowing down the process, and allowing the person to contemplate the feedback before absorbing it.

Sometimes judgments are right on target. They may point out a blind spot – which you need others to see. After all, by definition you cannot see your own blind spot. Other times judgments do not ring true. These may be projections.

I saw this distinction clearly during a particular event in my own life.

When I was a newlywed, I was working with a group where we were discussing balance. I shared some details of my work schedule and its travel requirements.

After the event concluded I was at a cocktail party. One of the attendees of the group approached me. He asked, "Are you open for some feedback?" (Details coming in *Guideline 12, I Will Ask Permission Before Offering Feedback*). I smiled, pleased that he was already using the tools. "Yes," I replied, "I am committed to curiosity."

"*Plexiglas* up," the attendee said. Now I knew he was serious. "This is just my judgment," he prefaced. "I'm concerned about your travel schedule," he said. "I think that it's damaging your relationship."

I appreciated him for the feedback and let it rest on my *Plexiglas*. The feedback concerned me – it was in my blind spot. Honoring this person's confidentiality, a week or so later I raised the topic of my travel schedule with my husband as a concern I had developed. He agreed with the feedback I had received: my travel was excessive for our relationship.

I pulled the feedback through my *Plexiglas*. I made some changes in my life, especially my travel schedule.

Months later, a similar situation occurred. In the context of a meeting, I mentioned my travel schedule. After the event, an attendee approached me. "Are you open for some feedback?" Again, I felt pleased to be practicing the tools. "Yes," I replied, committing to curiosity. "*Plexiglas* up," she said. "Just my judgment," she began. "I'm concerned that your travel schedule is damaging your relationship."

I appreciated the woman for offering me her feedback. I felt sad as I received the feedback for the second time, which I owned as my emotional experience. And I felt glad for the *Plexiglas*, which slowed the feedback down so I could consider it. It was not necessarily true – just a judgment, which allowed me to consider the feedback with curiosity.

Like the prior time, I let some time pass to honor the individual's confidentiality. I asked my husband again about my work travel commitments. He said that the agreements we had made before were still working for him. My travel wasn't his favorite thing, but it was not detrimental to our relationship.

This time, I let the feedback slide off the other side of my *Plexiglas*. I felt grateful for the reminder to pay attention. And I realized this time the feedback wasn't for me. I found out later that the woman who had given me the feedback was traveling to the detriment of her relationship. From a place of caring she offered me her feedback. This time it was a projection. It was true for her; it wasn't true for me.

As these examples show, when the first person owns the judgment, "Just my judgment," the person receiving the feedback more easily shifts to curiosity. In this open, candid environment, people share feedback. It lands on the *Plexiglas* allowing the other to consider it with curiosity. If it resonates, the person can act on the feedback. If it does not ring true, there still may be a lesson to learn, and the feedback can slide off the other side of the *Plexiglas*.

As you are likely starting to see, many guidelines become interdependent. By combining, *I will speak my truth* with *I will listen with curiosity,* my judgment (like my truth) becomes more valuable to my team members as well as more willingly received.

9

TAKE-AWAY

Judgments are just judgments, they are not facts. Offer them without being *right*. Receive others' judgments on your *Plexiglas*. They may or may not be true.

DISCUSSION QUESTIONS

• What risks do you perceive in sharing your judgments?

• What judgments do you have about yourself?

• What feedback do you have for others on this team?

I Will Own
My Feelings

Similar to owning judgments, owning your feelings *as
your own* is important for effective groups. I hear on a
regular basis that people hold back their true thoughts
because they are afraid of hurting someone else's feelings.
In reality, though, you are more likely to hurt someone
else's feelings through withholding than you are through
honest, constructive feedback.

I can say with confidence that *only the person experiencing
the emotion controls that feeling.* The reason is that I have
given the same piece of feedback to many different people
and they all reacted differently. The Center for Creative
Leadership has done studies with the same result: the
person having the feeling, not the person giving feedback,
determines feelings.

Being told that your report did not go out to the client could make you feel...

Embarrassed *(what was wrong with it?)*

Angry *(it was supposed to go out – what happened?)*

Scared *(am I going to get fired over this?)*

Relieved *(I get another chance to look it over)*

Appreciative *(I get to learn something new about my client and reporting system)*

Depending on your specific situation and how you interpret the information, you might even have a different reaction than any of those listed here.

Given this knowledge about feelings, respect and tact are still important values for a team. And, the ability to speak candidly (not brutally) provides more value than hiding the truth beneath "sugar coating." How to give feedback in a caring and healthy way is discussed in more detail in guidelines 11 and 12.

Another way that I have seen people not own their feelings is when they use "you" or "we" when they really mean "I." It dilutes the power of a statement. For example, notice the difference in the impact of these two stories:

A. You know when you get bad news about someone you care about and you don't know what to do?

B. When I got bad news about someone I care about recently, I felt scared and stuck. I didn't know what to do.

Similarly:

A. You know how others' suggestions feel like mandates and you feel like you have to do them, even if they're wrong?

B. I'm having a hard time differentiating suggestions from mandates. I feel confused and torn, like I have to implement them, even if I think they are wrong.

There is little action a person can take based on either of the first statements (version A). It's unclear if they are requests or general descriptions. In contrast, in each second statement, the person is taking responsibility. From this position, they might make a request or suggestion on a change to be made. With specificity and personalization in each of the second examples, the person making the statement is more likely to learn something new.

The substitution of "you" instead of "I" can lead to confusion. Additionally, it can lead to a feeling of ganging-up or group agreement that may not be reflective of the situation. "Even though it's risky, we think that's a good idea," is both more distant and sounds more definitive than "I think that's a good idea, and implementing it scares me." Unless you know what the other people think or feel, it's best to use "I." And if you want to be as powerful as possible, use "I" whenever feasible.

You may be worried that if you speak for yourself using "I" that you will be perceived as narcissistic or arrogant.

My experience is the opposite. When you speak from the "I" the clarity of your language lets people relax, knowing that you speak for yourself (not them) and they can do the same. Rather than the implicit arrogance that others agree with whatever you say, or that your experiences are the same, the language is clear. Each person speaks for himself or herself.

The most important application of the guideline *I will own my feelings* is the ability to identify and take responsibility for your emotional state. Schools teach students many things – math, history, English, etc. – but emotional intelligence is (sadly, in my judgment) not taught in most schools. Few leaders in any realm, therefore, feel comfortable navigating emotional conversations or situations. Despite the lack of training, managers estimate that they spend more than a quarter of their time addressing emotions that impede projects.

There are many complete books dedicated to the topic of feelings and emotional intelligence. For now, I'll give you a list of the most common emotions. Even being able to name an emotion from a list helps steer a person or team through the experience.

While the definition of primary emotions varies by expert, the emotions I see most commonly expressed in workplaces are anger, sadness, fear, joy and shame. Each emotion has a broad range of expression from "slight" to "overpowering."

Below is a chart to help sort various degrees of emotions into their primary emotion:

Anger
....
Mad • Irritated • Frustrated • Livid

Sadness/Grief
....
Sad • Upset • Disappointed • Depressed

Fear
....
Scared • Nervous • Worried • Terrified

Joy
....
Happy • Pleased • Grateful • Inspired

Shame
....
Stupid/Dumb • Embarrassed • Humiliated

The guideline *I will own my feelings* does not mean that you must stew or wallow in your emotions. Quite the contrary. Be clear about who is responsible for the feeling (you are in charge of your own feelings) and report them ("I feel angry about that") and you will lead the group through the emotion and into whatever needs to happen next: a release of the emotion, an apology, a break, problem-solving, or moving on to the next subject. Your ability to identify your own feeling and express it as just a feeling you are having is very powerful. You can own it as your current (temporary) experience.

TAKE-AWAY

<u>You</u> determine how you feel and how you address your feelings.

DISCUSSION QUESTIONS

- Which emotion do you experience most readily?

- Which feeling is the most difficult for you to notice in yourself?

- What are you feeling right now?

I Will Not Blame, Shame, or Fix Others

Whenever something doesn't go as planned, you may be tempted to blame someone else. You might feel like the victim, that what's happening isn't your fault. Especially if the group dynamic isn't what you'd hoped, you might find the person preventing it from reaching your ideal. When I work with teams, they usually say that blaming and complaining drain a lot of their energy.

In this guideline we group blame, shame and fixing into one. The reason is that as soon as blame shows up, the other two follow close behind. In any group where feedback is offered, there can be an allure to fix another person. You might think you have a great idea, or want to show off being smart. In blaming or fixing, it is very easy to shame another person. All three of these actions – blaming, shaming and fixing – avoid healthy responsibility and empowerment.

The first element of this guideline is to avoid blame and to instead take responsibility for the outcome. It is true that some things are out of your control (whether it rains, how another person feels, whether an idea is successful). Even so, powerful performers – from entry level to the CEO – take full responsibility for what happens, whatever that is. For example, if it rains, a person could blame the weatherman for a lousy forecast or just bad luck. A person taking responsibility might instead say, "I take responsibility for not being prepared for the rain. It's up to me to figure out how to stay dry, or to accept being wet."

Each time you complain, or feel "It's not my fault," you lose an opportunity to learn. You have a part to play in every circumstance of your life. When you can say, "I wonder how I contributed to this," you have stepped into responsibility and away from victimhood and blame. You reach your potential only when you stop blaming.

The second action to avoid is shaming someone else. We have already established that you are in charge of your own feelings. Everyone else is in charge of theirs, too. Shaming someone is telling them, "You are bad." This is different from expressing, "I disagreed with something you did." It is also different from, "Something you did was not what I expected or what I would have done." Shaming someone is making a negative character judgment about who they are as a person. For instance, "Your inability to finish this project proves that you are incompetent. You're worthless."

To avoid shaming, you can return to stating facts and owning judgments. "The facts are that the project isn't finished. My judgment is that you don't have what this project needs." As we saw with *I will speak my truth,* powerful leaders will take it to the next step: "I feel sad that I don't know how to make this work."

In the last guideline, I argued that you cannot make someone feel anything. You are in charge of your own feelings. Intentionally dishonoring or humiliating someone is another level. This damages morale of the group, impacting the safety to *speak your truth, ask for what you want,* or share a feeling. If you see someone else shamed, you will most likely avoid being vulnerable to prevent the same kind of embarrassment. This eliminates innovation and creativity as you stick to topics and ideas that are preapproved or perceived as safe by the group.

The last thing to avoid is fixing others. Sometimes a person asks for feedback. The next guideline addresses that situation. The guideline *I will not blame, shame or fix others* is about a frame of mind. It is easy to listen to someone's problem and immediately "solve" it for them. It is often driven by wanting to feel smart, or an obsession with being right. While it might provide some temporary relief, fixing prevents that person from thinking on their own. To create a truly successful team, it is much more powerful to coach a person to his or her own solution than to give them an answer.

In my experience, the resolution you have for yourself is much better than anything I could have given you. This makes sense because you know yourself and your situation better than I ever could.

GOOD QUESTIONS TO ASK A PERSON WHILE COACHING THEM INSTEAD OF FIXING THEM:

What do you want to have happen?

What do you really want? (See *Guideline 6, I will ask for what I want*)

How do you feel about this issue? (See *Guideline 10, I will own my feelings*)

What options do you have?

What are the benefits and risks of each option?

If you were advising someone else in your situation, what would you counsel them to do?

What support (resources, encouragement, etc.) **do you need to get what you want?**

You will certainly have other questions that are right for the moment or the situation. This list is meant to get you started.

The other reason to avoid fixing people is that it creates a guarded team culture, where it is difficult to bring an open-ended question or a topic to explore. People often resist sharing a dilemma because they don't want to be fixed. They just want help accessing their own creativity or innovation. When you coach instead of fixing, these topics come forward, and the entire team can learn alongside the individual who raised the topic.

11

You create openness and learning
when you take responsibility and coach
instead of blame, shame and fix.

DISCUSSION QUESTIONS

- When have you felt blamed, shamed or fixed? How did you react?

- When do you blame, shame or fix?

- What could you do instead?

12

I Will Ask Permission
Before Offering Feedback

In the last guideline I mentioned that sometimes you will have advice for people about their situations. Or, sometimes when a person is behaving a certain way, you might have a judgment about that behavior (which you would own, of course). Think of the last time someone gave you feedback. Did you receive it with openness and curiosity or with defensiveness? When you ask permission before offering feedback, you increase exponentially the probability that the other person will receive your comments with curiosity.

When I ask groups which guideline is most different from everyday life, most reply that asking permission before offering feedback would be the most dramatic change. This is good news because it's so easy. It requires a two-second phrase: "Are you open for some feedback?" So long as the intention is to solicit permission, alternative phrasing works as well. You might ask, "Can I challenge you on that?" or "Would you be open to a different perspective?" Even, "I have some thoughts for you on that if you'd like them."

The discipline is to hold back on the feedback if the person says they don't want it. This is crucial because the guideline only works if the person about to receive feedback has the authority to delay or refuse it. Again, it is only effective if the person says "Yes" to receive it.

When I ask permission before offering my observations or thoughts, 90% of the time (maybe even more often), the other person says, "Yes!" The added advantage is that of this 90% acceptance rate, the vast majority of the feedback is received with curiosity, especially for those practicing *I will listen with curiosity*. It may not be acted upon – that's their choice after they filter it on their *Plexiglas*; but the feedback is received with interest.

When a person gives feedback without asking permission, it often creates a feeling of hierarchy. The person giving the advice is asserting, "I know" and positioning the other as, "You don't know." Especially in peer situations, but even with bosses and subordinates, this power differential creates friction. Asking, "Are you open for some feedback?" gives the other person a chance to decide. This levels the playing field and evens the power between the people. The person giving the feedback agrees to give the feedback; the person receiving feedback agrees to receive it with curiosity. They both enter the agreement as partners in learning.

Once the person has agreed to the feedback, a few phrases that invite receptivity and shared learning are:

"You might consider …"

"From my experience …"

"What's worked well for me …"

"A possible option might be to …"

Sharing from your own experience keeps the feedback approachable. It does not blame, shame or fix, it just offers another perspective, which the person can incorporate into his thinking or her actions.

In the 10 percent of occasions when I ask a person, "Are you open?" and they say, "No," a few things may be happening beneath the surface. Perhaps the other person has received enough feedback. By the time it gets to be my turn, they are full. Perhaps they notice that they are starting to feel defensive and want to wait until another time so they get full benefit from my feedback. It could be that they are not interested in my personal opinion on a subject.

Most commonly, the person has begun to feel emotion. If, for whatever reason, the person chooses not to tip over into that emotion, they might request that I keep my feedback to myself – at least for the time being. Whatever the reason, I show that person tremendous respect by taking a deep breath and honoring their request to hold my suggestion.

"No," is a great opportunity for both of us to learn about what is keeping my perspective from being valuable to them. I might explore my own projections *(what about my suggestion to them applies to me?)*. I might write the feedback down for another time or place. Or I might drop the feedback entirely.

In many respects, *asking for permission before offering feedback* reminds the other person of their commitment to *receive feedback with curiosity and openness*. It allows them to *take care of themselves* in determining if now is the right moment for them to get more feedback. Asking permission also acknowledges that you are conscious that you are speaking your truth and not the truth, while *owning your judgments*. As you can see, this guideline requires the underlying use of many other guidelines.

TAKE-AWAY

By asking for permission before offering feedback, you increase the odds your feedback will be received with curiosity.

DISCUSSION QUESTION

• What would change in your group dynamic if you started asking each other permission before offering feedback?

I Forgive Myself and Others for Mistakes

Perhaps you are a perfectionist. Many successful leaders and managers self-identify as such. Others who have grown rapidly through an organization also pride themselves on their high attention to detail and a no-tolerance policy for mistakes.

On the one hand, this is admirable. Customers, clients and co-workers often greatly appreciate this commitment to excellence. On the other hand, if all mistakes are considered the enemy, you limit your ability to learn.

A willingness to acknowledge mistakes is an admission that no one is perfect. It is a commitment to yourself and the group that you will stretch yourself to take risks.

Any time you take a risk, chart new territory, or explore, you are bound to make a mistake. As Jazz drummer E.W. Wainwright once said, "A mistake is the most beautiful thing in the world. It's the only way to get somewhere you've never been before."

When these inevitable mistakes happen, this guideline encourages gentleness. It is still important to process the event and learn lessons so that the mistake does not happen again. (Note: The same mistake happening multiple times is a pattern, not a mistake.)

In groups that adopt this guideline, transparency increases dramatically. It becomes safe in the group to discuss failures and other mistakes – both big and small without blame and shame. It helps the team stay human. It helps individuals feel empowered to try something new. It helps the group grow deeper. When mistakes occur, make amends. Forgive anyone else involved. Forgive yourself. (It's usually harder!) Identify the lessons learned so that the mistake does not repeat. And move on to the next challenge.

So when you use these guidelines and find yourself defensive – laugh at being human, forgive yourself and commit again to curiosity. When you're late, or try to fix your entire group in one sitting, a healthy douse of self-forgiveness is in order.

And, finally, when you find that in some situations the guidelines conflict with each other - you'll have to forgive me for that mistake!

TAKE-AWAY

Nobody's perfect. Thank goodness for forgiveness.

DISCUSSION QUESTION

• What mistake do you need to forgive?

• What was the lesson learned?

Conclusion

These 13 guidelines are the secret to defining an atmosphere conducive to learning, creativity and success. Whether you participate in a YPO Forum, executive team, board, marriage, family, or writers' room you can adopt these guidelines to set the tone for your environment.

Underlying many of these guidelines is a shift to empowerment and responsibility. For many people, making this change is a challenge. These guidelines construct a context in which groups can together "take the plunge." Those who rise to the challenge find that the increase in candor, responsibility and authenticity results in more energy, creativity, success and fun.

Having just read *13 Guidelines*, you have the recipe for how to make your team move to the next level. Now you determine their success.

Start with yourself: how can you embody these guidelines on your team? In all areas of your life? By modeling these guidelines in your own actions, others are likely to be inspired to follow your lead. Review the takeaways at the end of each chapter on a regular basis until they feel second nature. Then, propose these as the guidelines for groups you participate in and the teams you lead. You can start by sharing the book. Or, have a discussion about each guideline using the questions at the end of each chapter. Be candid. Stay curious. Reach out for guidance or assistance if you need it.

With the help of these guidelines, you are on your way to an environment of trust, accountability, growth – and appreciation. Good luck!

About the Author

Kaley Warner Klemp is a sought-after facilitator, speaker and coach. She is an expert in small-group dynamics and leadership development, specializing in building trusting, synergistic teams that are able to achieve their strategic objectives – even in the face of challenging circumstances. Teams appreciate Kaley's interactive style and ability to translate theory into changes that last.

Kaley helps strengthen communication and conflict resolution skills as keys to improve performance. Since 2004, she has worked with executives and their teams to uncover and address the issues that block peak performance. Kaley helps teams foster a common vision, build trust, develop authentic relationships and use creative collaboration to achieve superior results. Once the leadership team is committed, Kaley compounds their gains by teaching communication and interaction skills throughout the organization.

A favorite with Young Presidents Organization (YPO) forums and chapters, Kaley has facilitated retreats for more than 175 member and spouse forums throughout the world. She has helped executive teams of some of the world's most prominent companies create cultures of responsibility and appreciation.

Kaley is a graduate of Stanford University, where she earned a B.A. in International Relations and an M.A. in Sociology, with a focus on Organizational Behavior. She is a certified yoga instructor and an avid athlete, spending time skiing, hiking, and mountain biking. She lives in Los Angeles, California with her husband Nate.

To find out more about Kaley, visit:
www.kaleyklemp.com

To order additional copies of this book, visit:
www.kaleyklemp.com/shop

Made in the USA
San Bernardino, CA
26 April 2018